Libraries Past and Present

by Kerry Dinmont

BUMBA BOOKS™

LERNER PUBLICATIONS ◆ MINNEAPOLIS

Note to Educators:

Throughout this book, you'll find critical thinking questions. These can be used to engage young readers in thinking critically about the topic and in using the text and photos to do so.

Lerner Publications Company
A division of Lerner Publishing Group, Inc.
241 First Avenue North
Minneapolis, MN 55401 USA

For reading levels and more information, look up this title at www.lernerbooks.com.

Library of Congress Cataloging–in–Publication Data

The Cataloging-in-Publication Data for *Libraries Past and Present* is on file at the Library of Congress.
ISBN 978-1-5415-0330-4 (lib. bdg.)
ISBN 978-1-5415-2689-1 (pbk.)
ISBN 978-1-5415-0778-4 (eb pdf)

Manufactured in the United States of America
1 – CG – 7/15/18

Table of Contents

Libraries through History

Libraries are places to learn and explore.

They have changed through history.

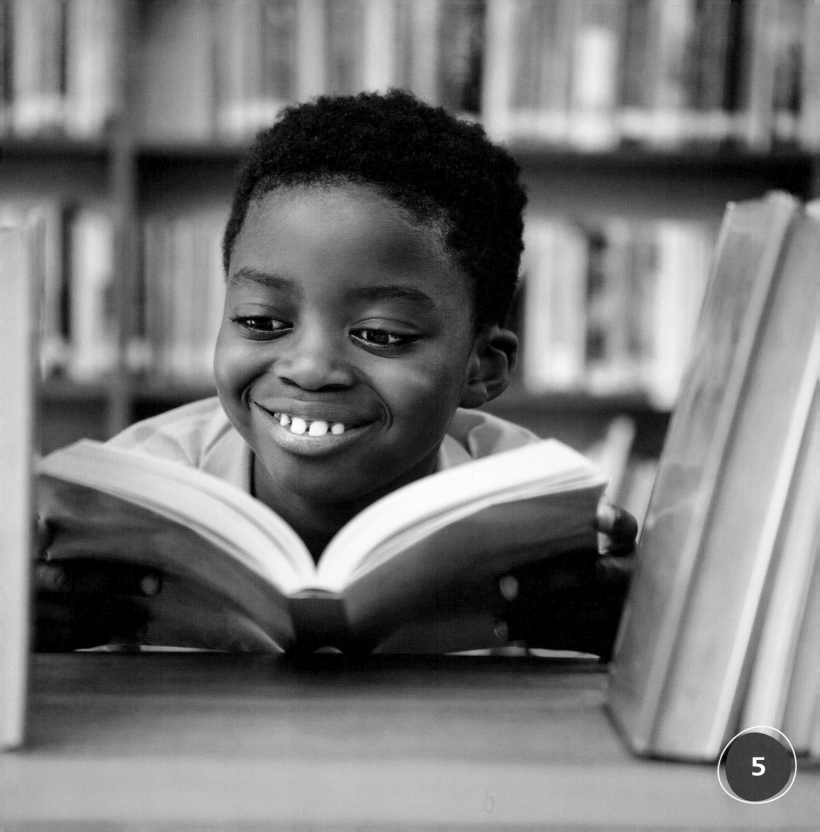

The first libraries held
only books.
These days, libraries also
have computers.
They have music and
magazines too.

What else
might you find
in a library?

Libraries used to be quiet.

People read and studied.

Now many libraries allow talking and playing. They have rooms for meetings.

Libraries had card catalogs.

Each book had a card.

The card said where to find that book.

Today the catalog is online.

You can look up books yourself.

Librarians still help you find what

you need.

Libraries have computers for anyone to use.

Libraries have e-books too.

Libraries have databases.

Databases let you find information

from experts.

When might you use a database?

Libraries have changed a lot.

But many things are still the same.

How do you use libraries?

Then and Now

Then

Libraries had books.

Libraries had card catalogs.

Libraries used to be quiet.

Today

Libraries have computers too.

The catalog is online.

Libraries have activities.

Picture Glossary

card catalogs

collections of cards with information about books

databases

collections of information from experts

e-books

books you can read on tablets and other devices

librarians

people who work in a library

23

Read More

Clark, Rosalyn. *A Visit to the Library*. Minneapolis: Lerner Publications, 2018.

Kenan, Tessa. *Hooray for Librarians!* Minneapolis: Lerner Publications, 2018.

Piehl, Janet. *Explore the Library*. Minneapolis: Lerner Publications, 2014.

Index

Photo Credits